Qatar
Travel Guide 2024

Use the Ultimate Travel Guide to Fully
Immerse Yourself in Culture, Cuisine, and
Adventure

D1374219

CORY R. HOBBS

Introduction

The fascinating country of Qatar is located in the center of the Arabian Gulf, where modernization and tradition coexist. This desert jewel invites adventurers to set out on a voyage unlike any other. It tells a story intertwined with the strands of ancient history and the glittering skyscrapers of modern marvels. Join us as we reveal the intricate story of Qatar, where urban landscapes paint visions of the future and dunes whisper stories of the past, from the bustling markets of Souq Waqif to the futuristic skyscrapers of Doha. Welcome to Qatar, a place where innovation and tradition mingle to entice you to immerse yourself in an enduring story where each step represents a new chapter just waiting to be explored.

Overview Qatar

Tucked away on the Arabian Peninsula's northeastern shore, Qatar offers an alluring fusion of modern and traditional elements. The country's cosmopolitan capital, Doha, presents a scene filled with golden dunes in the desert, antique souqs, and contemporary skyscrapers. Qatar, a country renowned for its rich cultural legacy, welcomes guests with open arms and provides a variety of experiences, from touring important historical sites like the Museum of Islamic Art to savoring the thriving food scene at Souq Waqif. Beyond the urban landscape, the tranquil waters of the Inland Sea and the distinctive mangrove ecosystems that round it reveal the natural splendor of Qatar. Qatar, a major international center of commerce and culture, welcomes visitors to experience an Arabian adventure where customs coexist peacefully with modernity. inventiveness.

Chapter One

Discovering [Qatar]

Exploring Qatar is akin to turning the pages of an antiquated book, where the story is revealed through layered traditions and inventiveness. Start your adventure in Doha, a city that skillfully combines the classic beauty of Souq Waqif with contemporary skyscrapers. See the Museum of Islamic Art, which stands proudly against the skyline, to learn about the beautiful patterns of Islamic art.

Go outside the municipal boundaries to see the swaying dunes of the desert and the everlasting splendor of the Inland Sea. Qatar's dedication to innovation and education is demonstrated by Education City, a global hub that attracts students from all over the world.

Explore the opulent Pearl-Qatar waterfront, an architectural wonder that resembles a string of pearls. Savor the fragrant charm of Karak tea while listening to the rhythmic pulse of Doha's bustling streets. And when the sun sets over the Arabian Gulf, allow Qatar to show itself as a place where folktales from the past collide with contemporary goals, beckoning you to join its dynamic narrative.

Chapter Two

Doha:

The Urban Center

Discover the vibrant city of Doha, where the skyline is adorned with soaring skyscrapers like the Torch Doha. Explore the lively Souq Waqif marketplaces and pay a visit to the magnificent Museum of Islamic Art, a shining example of Islamic cultural legacy. Don't miss the vibrant Corniche along the Arabian Gulf or the marvels of modern architecture.

Pearl-Qatar: Opulence by the Water

Set out to visit Pearl-Qatar, a man-made island studded with posh homes, fancy stores, and scenic marinas. Enjoy a luxurious and laid-back stroll around the glitzy waterfront.

Education City: The Oasis of Knowledge

Take in the intellectual oasis that is Education City, a center that hosts esteemed worldwide research institutes and universities. See how innovation and education converge in this special region of Qatar.

Al Thakira: Peace and Mangroves
Explore the calm splendor of Al Thakira, which is surrounded by vast mangrove forests. In this tranquil haven, commune with nature by taking a leisurely kayak tour of the mangroves or a leisurely stroll along the boardwalk.

Dunes and Desert Majesty in the Inland Sea
See the fascinating Inland Sea by traveling deep into the desert. A breathtaking scenery of immaculate dunes is what awaiting adventurers and those seeking the peace and quiet of the desert.

Al Wakrah: A Coastside History
Discover the historical allure of Al Wakrah, a heritage-rich seaside city. Explore the ancient Souq Al Wakrah and take in the lively atmosphere and traditional architecture.

The Katara Cultural Village: An Arts Tapestry
Come to Katara Cultural Village and immerse yourself in the arts and culture. This center houses performance spaces, galleries, and theaters, demonstrating Qatar's dedication to protecting and advancing its cultural legacy.

Every location of Qatar reveals a different aspect of this vibrant country, providing a wide variety of experiences ranging from contemporary luxury to the timeless appeal of the desert.

Chapter Three

Experiencing local culture

Souq Waqif: Explore the core of Qatari culture at Doha's Souq Waqif. With its traditional textiles, handicrafts, and scented spices, this lively market is a sensory feast. Enjoy traditional Qatari food, interact with local sellers, and take in live entertainment.

Participate in a traditional majlis, a sitting place where residents congregate to socialize, to experience the hospitality of Qatar. Talk to one other, tell each other tales, and sip Arabic coffee—a sign of coziness and welcome.

Attend cultural events and festivals, such the Doha Cultural Festival or the celebrations of Qatar National Day. These performances include traditional dance, music, and artwork, offering a colorful window into Qatar's rich past.

Dress in Traditional Attire: Wearing traditional Qatari clothing, such as the abaya for ladies and the thobe for men, will allow you to have a personal look at the culture. This shows respect for regional customs while also enabling you to fit in.

Folklore Dancing: Take in traditional dance performances, such as the Ardha dance, which symbolizes the togetherness of Qatar. These shows, which frequently occur at cultural events, provide insight into the proud traditions of the country.

Qatari Cuisine: Savor real Qatari food as you discover the region's gastronomic scene. Taste specialties like Harees (a wheat and meat dish) and Machboos (spicy rice with meat). To wash it all down, have a cup of sweetened Karak tea.

Traditional Arts & Crafts: Take a look at the traditional arts and crafts produced in Qatar in art galleries and craft stores.These artistic representations offer a deeper appreciation of the nation's cultural past, ranging from complex calligraphy to pottery.

Come experience the thrill of camel racing, a popular customary sport in Qatar. Visit a nearby racecourse to see these magnificent animals in action as they demonstrate the blending of history and modernity.

Participating in various facets of local life will help you develop a deep understanding of the diverse cultural fabric that makes up Qatar.

Chapter Four

Outdoor Adventures

Dune Bashing in the Desert: Drive a 4x4 car across the fascinating sand dunes in the vast desert to experience the exhilarating thrill of dune bashing. This journey combines the allure of the desert with thrilling experiences.

Sandboarding: Try sandboarding to take on the dunes in a novel manner. Experience the exhilarating thrill of snowboarding combined with the warmth of the desert sun as you glide down the sandy slopes.

Kayaking in Al Thakira Mangroves: Take a kayak tour through the calm waters of Al Thakira's mangroves. As you paddle through narrow canals, you'll be able to see a variety of bird species and take in the peace and quiet of this special coastal environment.

Safari by the Inland Sea: Experience a unique desert safari by visiting the Inland Sea. Admire the enormous stretches of immaculate sand dunes that meet the blue seas of the Arabian Gulf, providing an amazing setting for a once-in-a-lifetime experience.

Snorkeling on Banana Island: Take a trip to Banana Island and immerse yourself in the pristine waters for a snorkeling experience. Discover colorful coral reefs and a variety of aquatic life; this is an underwater enthusiast's dream come true.

Camping Under the Stars: When you camp beneath a blanket of stars, you can truly feel the magic of the desert night. Camping facilities are available in many places in Qatar, allowing you to take in the peace and beauty of the desert after dusk.

Jet Skiing along the Coast: Enjoy the wind's thrill as you glide down Qatar's stunning coast. For those who enjoy water sports, the coastal waters offer an exciting playground regardless of skill level.

Mountain Biking in Zekreet: Take a mountain bike ride through the area's distinctive rock formations and arid scenery. The difficult paths are thrilling and provide breathtaking vistas.

Fishing Trips: Take a trip to the Arabian Gulf and try your hand at capturing some of the local marine life. Enjoying your fresh catch afterwards makes it a satisfying and serene outdoor pastime.

Parasailing in Doha Bay: Take a thrilling parasailing experience and soar above the bay and the city skyline. Savor the thrill of soaring over the ocean while taking in expansive views of the city and the coast.

These outdoor experiences in Qatar offer the ideal balance of action, scenic beauty, and cultural discovery.

Chapter Five

Food and drinks

Machboos:
a tasty dish of perfectly cooked meat, usually chicken or lamb, served over spicy rice.

Harees: A hearty dish of pork and wheat that is slow-cooked until it becomes creamy.

Dates and Arabic Coffee (Gahwa): Start your meal with a robust, fragrant cup of Arabic coffee and some delicious dates, which are a staple of Qatari hospitality.

Kunafa: Indulge in the sweetness of this delightful treat, which is formed of thin pastry that resembles noodles and is soaked in a syrup made of sugar.

Global Tastes:

5. Savor the well-known street cuisine from the Middle East, shawarma, which consists of marinated meat that is thinly sliced and wrapped in flatbread.

Falafel: Enjoy falafel, which is made of deep-fried fava or chickpea patties that can be eaten as a side dish or in wraps.

Mixed Grill: Treat yourself to a carnivorous feast of grilled veggies, kebabs, and various meats on a plate.
Superb Seafood Buffet:
8. Grilled Fish: Savor the freshness of fish that has been caught nearby, perfectly grilled, and seasoned with flavorful spices.

Qatari Fish Majboos: A seafood-inspired take on the traditional machboos, this dish consists of rice cooked with fish and aromatic spices.
Various Dining Occasions:
10. Nobu's Fine Dining Doha: Nobu, housed in the opulent Four Seasons Hotel Doha, offers top-notch Japanese-Peruvian fusion cuisine that will elevate your dining experience.

Street Food at Souq Waqif: Take in the lively ambiance of Souq Waqif while sampling the street food selection, which includes falafel and traditional desserts.

Drinks to Refresh:

12. Karak Tea: Sip into a cup of Karak, a spicy tea enhanced with condensed milk, and immerse yourself in Qatari tea culture.

Jallab: Made with grape molasses, dates, and rose water, Jallab is a delightful beverage that will quench your thirst.

Tamarind Juice: Savor the distinct taste of tamarind in a cool drink that's ideal for cooling off in Qatar's warm weather.

For food lovers, Qatar is a foodie's paradise, offering a delectable blend of traditional Qatari dishes, foreign flavors, and a wide variety of dining experiences.

Chapter Six

Practical travel tips

Visa Requirements: Sample the street food options at Souq Waqif, which includes falafel and traditional pastries, while taking in the lively atmosphere of the market.

Drinks that Revive:

12. Karak Tea: Savor a cup of the spiced tea, sweetened with condensed milk, and embrace the tea culture of Qatar.

Jallab: A cool beverage composed with dates, rose water, and grape molasses, Jallab will quench your thirst.

Taste the distinct flavor of tamarind in a cool drink that's ideal for quenching in Qatar's warm weather.

Food lovers will find heaven in Qatar, where the country's cuisine is a fascinating blend of local specialties, flavors from around the world, and a wide variety of eating options.

Currency: The national currency is the Qatari Riyal (QAR). Although most places accept credit cards, it's a good idea to have some local cash on hand, particularly for markets and smaller businesses.

Transportation: The transportation infrastructure in Qatar is advanced. There is an effective public transit system and plenty of taxis to choose from. Another practical choice for traveling outside of the city is to rent a car.

Health precautions: Make sure you are informed of the local medical services and that you have travel insurance. Although bottled water is easily accessible, tap water is usually safe.

Cultural Sensitivity: Pay attention to regional traditions, particularly in the month of Ramadan. During the day, stay away from eating, drinking, and smoking in public.

Safety:

Travelers usually believe Qatar to be safe. Be mindful of your surroundings, use the usual safety precautions, and abide by local laws.

Time Zone: UTC+3 Arabian Standard Time (AST) is used in Qatar. Make sure to check the time in your area before scheduling any appointments or activities.

Local SIM Card: To enable your phone to access local services and data, think about purchasing a local SIM card. Wi-Fi is commonly accessible in public areas and hotels.

Public Place Etiquette: Always act with respect when in public areas. Keep your voice down and be aware of regional traditions, particularly when it comes to prayer times.

Mall stores usually open in the morning, close for a few hours in the afternoon, and then reopen in the evening. Souks, or traditional markets, may have varying hours of operation.

Emergency Contacts: Store in your phone the local emergency numbers of the police, ambulance, and consulates of your nation.

You may optimize your trip and make the most of your time in Qatar by adhering to these useful travel suggestions.

Chapter Seven

Accommodations

The St. Regis Doha:
A sumptuous hotel on the waterfront with luxurious accommodations, fine restaurants, and a private beach.

Doha's Four Seasons Hotel: Experience first-rate service, luxurious amenities, and rooms with a view of the sea at this elegant hotel.

Boutique Style:

The Al Najada Doha Hotel by Tivoli is a boutique hotel in Souq Waqif that combines contemporary comforts with traditional architectural design from Qatar.

The Avenue, a Murwab Hotel: This boutique hotel offers a distinctive fusion of design and individualized service and is centrally located in Doha.

Cost-effective Choices:

La Villa Hotel: An affordable choice close to the airport with cozy lodging and standard amenities.

Ezdan Hotel: Popular with budget tourists, Ezdan Hotel offers reasonably priced rooms in a handy location.
Resorts for Unwinding:

Experience peace and quiet at Sharq Village & Spa, a Ritz-Carlton hotel. This beachside resort features traditional architecture and a spa.
Anantara's Banana Island Resort Doha: Get away to an opulent island resort featuring a variety of leisure activities and overwater villas.
Apartments with services:

Fraser Suites Doha: Providing completely furnished apartments with hotel-quality amenities, Fraser Suites is perfect for extended stays.
Combining the comforts of apartment living with the extras of a five-star hotel is the Mövenpick Hotel West Bay Doha.

Business Vacationers:

The W Doha Hotel & Residences is a hotel that caters to business travelers and offers contemporary amenities in a lively ambiance.

Mondrian Doha: An elegant hotel ideal for business travels, featuring conference and event spaces.

amiable Allowances:

The Marriott Marquis City Center Doha Hotel is a great choice for families because it has large rooms, a pool, and easy access to stores.

Oryx Rotana Doha: Known for its welcoming environment for families, Oryx Rotana provides a variety of food options and leisure amenities.

Ancient Charm:

Situated next to Msheireb Downtown Doha, the Alwadi Hotel Doha - MGallery combines contemporary elegance with its ancient surroundings.

Think about your preferences when selecting a place to stay in Qatar, whether they are for luxury, convenience to attractions, or a more affordable choice. Qatar provides a wide range of variety of resorts and hotels to accommodate different traveler demands and tastes.

Chapter Eighth

Day trips and excursions

Discover the UNESCO World Heritage site that is the old Zubarah Fort, and get a taste of traditional Qatari life by visiting the nearby seaside village of Al Ruwais.
Safari via Inland Sea:

Visit the Inland Sea (Khor Al Adaid), where towering sand dunes meet the glistening Arabian Gulf, for an exhilarating desert adventure.
Village Cultural Katara:

Visit Katara Cultural Village for a day to see the traditional architecture, theaters, and art galleries of Qatar. Savor cultural events and views of the waterfront.
The Islamic Art Museum and the Corniche Walk:

Start the day with a trip to Doha's Museum of Islamic Art, then take a leisurely stroll down the charming Corniche.

Dukhan and Film City:
Visit Film City, a neighboring set that is modeled after an ancient Arabian village, when you travel to Dukhan, a town renowned for its natural beauty.
Investigation of North Qatar:

Explore the northern areas of Qatar, such as the mangrove-filled Al Khor, the kayak-friendly Al Thakira, and the archaeological site of Al Zubara.
Resort at Sealine Beach:

Savor the beach, dune buggy rides, or a camel ride while unwinding at Sealine Beach Resort. It's the ideal getaway location, close to Doha.
Industrial Mesaieed City:

Experience the calm Sealine Beach and Qatar's industrial scenery by taking a tour to Mesaieed Industrial City.

Discover the Sheikh Faisal Bin Qassim Al Thani Museum, which features a sizable collection of objects and artwork from all around the world. Villaggio Mall and Aspire Park:

After spending a fun-filled family day at Aspire Park, visit Villaggio Mall, one of Qatar's biggest shopping centers, for shopping and entertainment.
Explore the bustling Al Wakrah Souq for traditional Qatari items, take a stroll along the Corniche, and visit the old city of Al Wakrah.
Explore the Qatar National Library and the other educational establishments that contribute to Qatar's knowledge environment by spending a day in Education City.

To help you make the most of your stay in Qatar, these day tours and excursions provide a variety of experiences, from cultural exploration to desert adventures.

Chapter Nine

Discover Souq Waqif's lesser-known nooks and crannies, where artisanal stores and hidden eateries provide a more personal experience away from the busy main streets.
Sunset in Al Bidda Park:

Experience a magnificent sunset in Al Bidda Park, a calm haven in the middle of Doha that provides the ideal get-away from the bustle of the city.
Local Dining Options in Al Wakrah:

Explore Al Wakrah's tourist attractions and find real, neighborhood restaurants that serve genuine Qatari cuisine. The possibilities for seafood are very delicious.
Unbeaten Path Sand Dunes:

Avoid the crowds and venture into lesser-known dune areas for a more private desert experience. travel routes. Savor the peace and quiet of the desert environment.

Cultural Occasions at Katara:

For information on upcoming performances, art exhibits, and cultural festivals, check out the Katara Cultural Village event calendar. It serves as a gathering place for those who love culture.

Local Gallery Exhibitions:

See independent art galleries that feature the creations of up-and-coming local and foreign artists in Msheireb Downtown Doha and The Pearl-Qatar.

Eating in Porto Arabia at The Pearl-Qatar:

Discover the rich and varied gastronomic landscape of Porto Arabia at The Pearl-Qatar. Here, you'll find undiscovered treasures offering a wide range of world cuisines.

Exclusive Camps in the Desert:
For a more customized and close-knit experience with the desert environment, think about setting up a private desert camp.
Activities for the Community at Education City:

Participate in community events and talks in Education City to network with a varied audience and learn about a range of topics.
Local Associations for Water Sports:

Make contact with neighborhood water sports organizations to enjoy more genuine experiences with sports like sailing, paddleboarding, and kayaking, particularly at Al Thakira.
Take a Boat Tour of the Mangroves:

For a unique viewpoint and a tranquil excursion, consider taking a boat tour through the mangroves of Al Thakira in instead of a usual kayaking experience.

Join Local Meetup Groups:

Join local meetup groups by using social media channels. This is a fantastic method to find events and things to do, as well as make connections with other expats and locals.

For those who are prepared to go off the beaten route, these insider's recommendations offer a glimpse into the more complex and lesser-known aspects of Qatar, offering a more genuine and in-depth experience.

Chapter Ten

Travel resources

Qatar Tourism:
Extensive details about travel necessities, events, and sights can be found on the official tourism website.

Travel guides: Lonely Planet - Qatar: A trustworthy resource for guides that include information on accommodations, points of interest, and regional customs.

Platforms for booking accommodations: Booking.com: Provides a large selection of hotels, condos, and resorts in Qatar along with competitive pricing and customer reviews.

Platforms for booking flights: Skyscanner: Evaluate airfares and discover the most affordable flights to Qatar from many airlines.

Travel Forums:

Consult other travelers' experiences and recommendations who have been to or are intending to visit Qatar in the TripAdvisor - Qatar Forum.

Apps for Local Transportation:

The Karwa Taxi App offers trustworthy and convenient taxi services in Qatar.

Stay informed about Doha's railway and metro services with Qatar Rail.

Information about the weather:

Qatari weather reported by BBC: Verify the current weather and forecasts for the days you want to travel.

Calendars of Cultural Events: Events at Katara Cultural Village: Be updated about exhibitions, performances, and other cultural events.

Currency Converter: XE Currency Converter: Keep abreast of current exchange rates, particularly if you'll be traveling with multiple currencies.

- **Language translation apps:**
- Google Translate is helpful for speaking in several languages and translating menus and signs.

- **Local SIM Card Providers:**
- Look into prepaid SIM cards from nearby telecom companies like Ooredoo and Vodafone, as they can provide reasonably priced calling and data plans.

- **Travel Insurance Companies:**
- Global Nomads To be sure you're covered for unforeseen circumstances throughout your vacation, think about getting travel insurance.

-
- **World Health Organization (WHO) - Qatar:**
- Health and Safety Information Keep yourself updated on health-related news and any advisories regarding travel.

- You can maximize your time in Qatar by using these resources to plan your trip, be informed, and get the most out of it.

Conclusion

May the fusion of antiquated customs and cutting-edge wonders unfold before you like a gripping tale as you travel to Qatar. From the vibrant Souq Waqif markets to the tranquil waters of the Inland Sea, Qatar welcomes you to explore a country where modern innovation and cultural diversity coexist peacefully.

Savor the variety of flavors found in Qatari cuisine, discover hidden jewels that are only known to insiders, and lose yourself in the kind hospitality of the people. Whether you're walking through the colorful streets of Doha or negotiating the dunes of the desert, every time you spend in Qatar offers an opportunity to get to know a country that skillfully combines its past, present, and future.

Your voyage is set to be a tapestry of experiences with a wealth of resources at your disposal, insider recommendations, and helpful travel advice. Now, venture forth and succumb to the charm of Qatar—a place where the sounds of the past collide with the beats of modernity, beckoning you to participate in its always changing story. Happy travels!

Made in United States
North Haven, CT
27 January 2024

47951857R00024